PASSOVER

BY CATHY GOLDBERG FISHMAN
ILLUSTRATIONS BY JENI REEVES

On My Own

HOLIDAYS

M Millbrook Press/Minneapolis

The illustrator would like to thank the members of Temple Judah in Cedar Rapids, Iowa, who took part in this book. I am especially grateful to Barbara and Steven Feller for their enthusiastic support. To them and the rest of the models for Passover, Brian and Tessa Cohen; Charles, Kathryn, and Curtis Litow; Faith and Melanie Abzug; Phillip Underwood; and Heidi Feller, I thank you all for enlightening me.

Millbrook Press
A division of Lerner Publishing Group
241 First Avenue North
Minneapolis, MN 55401 U.S.A.

Website address: www.lernerbooks.com

Library of Congress Cataloging-in-Publication Data

Fishman, Cathy Goldberg.
    Passover / by Cathy Goldberg Fishman ; illustrations by Jeni Reeves.
      p.   cm. — (On my own holidays)
    ISBN-13: 978–1–57505–656–2 (lib. bdg. : alk. paper)
    ISBN-10: 1–57505–656–9 (lib. bdg. : alk. paper)
    1. Passover—Juvenile literature. [1. Passover. 2. Holidays.] I. Marshall, Ann, 1976–
ill. II. Title. III. Series.
BM695.P3F58 2006
296.4'37—dc22   2003021046

Manufactured in the United States of America
1 2 3 4 5 6 – JR – 11 10 09 08 07 06

To Mae Frances Leverett, with love
—C.G.F.

To friend and photographer, Roz Tepper-Byrne
—J.R.

Every spring, Jewish people all over
the world gather together
for a holiday called Passover.
On Passover, Jews remember a time
when they were slaves in Egypt.
They remember their escape from slavery.
And they remember the gift of freedom.

The story of Passover
is written in the Hebrew Bible.
It happened in Egypt
about three thousand years ago.
The Jewish people were called Israelites,
or the Children of Israel.

The king of Egypt was called Pharaoh.
He ruled over the Israelites
and made them into slaves.
Pharaoh commanded them to build cities
with bricks made from mud and straw.
He made their lives very hard.

The Israelites suffered

for many years.

They dreamed of a day

when they would be free.

They cried out to their God for help.

Finally, God sent them a brave

Israelite man.

His name was Moses.

God commanded Moses to be

a strong voice for his people.

Moses went to Pharaoh.

"Let my people go!" he demanded.

But Pharaoh said no.

He did not want to give up

his valuable slaves.

Moses warned Pharaoh that

the Israelite God was very powerful.

Moses said that God would punish

Pharaoh and the Egyptian people.

But Pharaoh would not listen.

God brought down a disaster called a plague.

This plague turned all the water
in Egypt into blood.

The Egyptian people suffered.

But Pharaoh did not care.

He still would not free
the Israelites.

Moses went back to Pharaoh many times. Each time, Pharaoh refused to free the Israelites. And each time, the God of the Israelites sent a new plague to Egypt.

Some of the plagues harmed
the Egyptian people.
Some of the plagues hurt their animals
and their land.
But Pharaoh had a hard heart.
The first nine plagues did not change him.

Moses spoke to Pharaoh for one last time.

He told Pharaoh

to let the Israelites go.

But Pharaoh still said no.

Then Moses warned him

about one last plague.

Moses said this 10th plague would be

the most horrible of all.

This plague would kill the firstborn son

in every Egyptian family.

Moses ran back to the Israelites
with a message from God.
He warned them about the last plague.
He told each Israelite family to paint
marks over their doors
with the blood of a lamb.

The plague would not enter any house
with this mark.
It would pass over the house instead.
Moses also told the Israelites to roast
the lamb and eat it that night.
It would be the first Passover dinner.

At midnight, the horrible plague came
to every Egyptian home.
But the plague passed over the homes
of the Israelites.
Pharaoh could hear his people crying.

Even Pharaoh's first son died.

Pharaoh's heart changed.

He called for Moses that night.

Pharaoh wanted the plagues to stop.

He told Moses to take the Israelite people
and leave Egypt.

Moses and the Israelites quickly packed
their belongings.
They took their clothing, their cattle,
and their sheep.
They took food for the long journey.
But there was no time to bake bread.
They packed raw dough instead.

The Children of Israel followed Moses
toward freedom.
They walked and walked.
Then they stopped to rest and eat.

They baked their bread dough
in the desert heat.
The dough baked hard and flat.
The Israelites called it matzah.

Moses led the Israelites
to the Sea of Reeds to rest again.
They were getting farther and farther
from Pharaoh.
But Pharaoh's heart had changed again.
He wanted his slaves back.
He was chasing after them
with soldiers and horses.

The Israelites saw Pharaoh
coming after them.
They could not go forward.
The sea was too wide and deep.
The Israelites could not turn back.
Pharaoh and his soldiers were
right behind them.
The Israelites were trapped and afraid.
They cried out to Moses for help.

Moses gave his people
a message from God.
March forward into the sea!

The Israelites were frightened.
But they listened to Moses.
They marched into the deep water.
Then a strong wind began to blow.
It blew the water apart.
The wind made a dry path
for the Israelites.
The Israelites walked along the path
to the other side of the sea.

Pharaoh's soldiers ran after the Israelites.

The soldiers marched onto the dry path

in the middle of the sea too.

But the wind stopped blowing.

The water in the Sea of Reeds

came back together.

The soldiers drowned.

The Israelites were safe.

They sang and danced.

They thanked God for their freedom.

They promised to remember the pain
of Pharaoh's cruel ways.

They promised to be kind to other people.

And they promised to always tell their
children the story of their escape.

Today, the Jewish people celebrate
Passover each year to remember
the story of their freedom.
Passover comes in March or April.
But it always begins on the 15th of Nisan,
the seventh month of the Jewish year.
Many Jews observe Passover for eight days.

Many Jewish families get ready
for Passover before the holiday begins.
They clean their houses.
They buy special food for Passover.
During Passover, many families
eat matzah instead of bread.
They also eat other foods
made just for Passover.
The matzah and other foods help Jews
remember their escape from slavery.

On the first night of Passover,
Jewish families have a seder.
At this special meal,
they remember the story of Passover.
They read the story in a book
called the Haggadah.

The Haggadah also has blessings,
prayers, and songs.
One person at the table usually
leads the seder.
But in many homes,
everyone at the seder takes turns
reading the Haggadah out loud.

A beautiful seder plate sits on the table.
The seder plate holds food that reminds
the Jewish people of the Passover story.
Each food has a name in Hebrew,
the traditional language of the Jews.
Karpas is a green vegetable, such as parsley.
It is green like new life in spring.
It reminds Jewish people that the
Israelites were freed in the spring.
People at the seder dip the vegetable in
salty water to remember the slaves' tears.
Maror is bitter herbs.
People use horseradish or bitter lettuce.
It stands for the bitterness of slavery.
Charoset is a mixture
of chopped apples and nuts.
It looks like the mud and straw
that the Israelites used to make bricks.

Zeroa is a roasted bone.

It stands for the lamb the Israelites

roasted for their first Passover dinner.

Beitzah is a roasted egg.

The egg stands for spring and new life.

The seder plate doesn't hold
all the food at a seder.
Three pieces of matzah are wrapped
in a beautiful cloth.
Matzah reminds the Jewish people of
the matzah they ate long ago in Egypt.
It is hard and flat.
During the seder, the leader takes the
middle piece of matzah out of the cloth.
The leader breaks the matzah in half
and hides part of it.
The hidden matzah is called
the afikomen.
It is the last thing that everyone will eat
at the seder.

There are wine cups on the table too.
Everyone at the seder drinks four cups
of wine or grape juice.
The wine and juice stand for
the joy of freedom.
The drink also helps Jewish people
remember the 10 plagues.
During the seder, the leader reads
about the plagues from the Haggadah.

Everyone dips a finger in the wine or
grape juice each time a plague is named.
They let the wine or juice drip
onto their napkin or plate.
Ten drops fall,
one for each plague.
The drops take away some of the joy
in each person's cup.
The drops stand for suffering that the
plagues caused the Egyptian people.

Jewish children have an important part
at the seder.
Each year, they read the same
Four Questions out of the Haggadah.
Usually, the youngest child reads
the Four Questions.
Sometimes all the children get a turn.
The questions are in Hebrew and English.
The first words are, "Why is this night
different from all other nights?"
The leader reads the answers
out of the Haggadah.
The Haggadah says that this night is
different to help Jews remember.
It helps them remember slavery
and the gift of freedom.

Soon it is time to eat the seder dinner.
Each Jewish family makes its favorite
Passover meal.
There is always plenty of food and talk
and laughter.

After the dinner, the leader reads
out of the Haggadah again.
Everyone sings the prayers and blessings.

Now it is time to find the afikomen.
In many homes, the children at the seder
hunt for the hidden piece of matzah.
They look under the chairs.
They look behind the doors.
The child who finds the afikomen
gets a present.

Everyone has a small taste
of the afikomen to end the seder.
The last part of the Haggadah says
that the seder is over.
People at the seder pray that they will
celebrate Passover next year too.
This seder is over.
But Passover is not over.
Many Jewish families have another seder
the next night.

Some Jewish families also go to
their synagogue during Passover.
And many Jews will eat only special
Passover food for the rest of the holiday.
Next year, they will gather together again.
They will remember how the Jewish
people became free.
And they will tell their children
how important freedom is
for everyone in the world.

Passover Words

afikomen (ah-fee-KOH-muhn): a piece of matzah that is hidden during the seder

beitzah (bay-TZA): a roasted egg on the seder plate that represents spring and new life

charoset (khah-ROH-set): usually a mixture of apples, nuts, and cinnamon that stands for the material Israelite slaves used to make bricks

Haggadah (hah gah DAH): a book used at the seder that tells the story of Passover

karpas (kahr-PAHS): usually parsley. It stands for spring.

maror (mah-ROHR): a bitter herb that stands for the bitterness of slavery

matzah (mat-ZAH): a hard, flat bread made from flour and water

Moses (MOH-zihs): the leader of the Israelites who led his people to freedom

Nisan (nee-SAHN): the seventh month in the Jewish calendar; in biblical terms, it is also known as the first month of the year.

Pharaoh (FAIR-oh): the king of the Egyptians

seder (SAY-dur): the special Passover dinner

zeroa (zeh-roh-AH): a roasted bone that stands for the lamb killed in the Passover story

Note on pronunciation: In Hebrew, the *ch* denotes a throaty *h* sound.